Let's Doodle

Fatima Alvarez

Juan Alvarez

Introduction

I would like to thank and congratulate you on purchasing this book. You will be able to improve your creativity by doodling and realize that it isn't only a "mindless" act, but rather a skill that everyone should utilize.

I remember doodling in class lectures and getting scolded for it when the teacher realized I "wasn't focused".

However, I always knew that it was helpful for me when I needed to memorize information in a short amount of time. I could either doodle and stay focused in class or pretend to pay attention and doze off.

After much research, I realized that I wasn't the only one benefiting from doodling since researchers have begun to understand how doodling works.

It turns out we become more engaged in the subject when we utilize two learning styles instead of just one.

By listening and doodling we can remain focused on the task at hand but retain more information due to the fact that the kinesthetic learning style is used in conjunction with the auditory.

The goal of this book is to bring you to the realization that doodling is helpful in improving the way you think and perform your daily activities. Once you practice doodling with the many prompts in this book, it will become easier for you to doodle on your own.

Sometimes we feel like drawing but we don't know what to draw. Doodling is a form of drawing, which isn't as strict and can be done effectively by anyone without much practice or supplies. After completing the prompts, you can apply them to any aspect of your life.

A few examples on the way you can apply doodling to your daily tasks include:

- Brainstorming
- Studying
- Note taking
- Stress relief
- Meetings
- Lectures
- Meeting new people
- Explaining ideas
- Problem solving
- Reflecting thoughts and ideas
- Enhancing creativity
- Just for fun!

...And much more!

Tips for using the prompts

This book is filled with creative prompts that will help unleash your imagination. As you approach each prompt, try to clear your mind and see where your doodle takes you.

Remember that these are fun exercises; you don't have to worry about perfection or complexity. Simply doodle what comes to mind, what you envision, or how you feel the prompt affects you. There is no right or wrong doodle!

Some prompts are designed to help you create doodles that represent different aspects of your life. Others make you think outside the box and will help you explore your imagination and bring out your untapped inner creativity. While yet others will allow you to fill in part of the prompt to give you even more flexibility.

It is recommended that you keep this book with you so that you are able to doodle whenever you feel the need to. Sometimes we are struck with sudden creativity that we need to immediately put down on paper, or we get the sudden urge to doodle.

By taking this book with you, you will also have all of your doodles in one place. It is great being able to look back at your previous doodles as your realize that you have become more creative and are able to see improvements in your technique. And you can find inspiration by looking through doodles that represent aspects of your life, reflect your goals, or reminds you of your accomplishments.

Remember to have fun with these prompts as you learn to create your own prompts later on. I hope you enjoy the doodling prompts and get as much out of it as we put in!

Prompts

Create a masterpiece out of your name

Create your own amusement park

What will you look like in 20 Years?

Doodle an imaginary animal

What makes you happy?

Favorite object you own

What makes you proud?

Create a complex doodle
with only circles

If you had one wish what would it be?

Your favorite memory from grade school

Your grumpy coworker

A stranger you encountered today

If you could purchase anything right now what would it be?

Doodle your favorite coffee mug

Create an abstract doodle using five different colors

Who is your favorite celebrity?

Create a decorative doodle to hang up in your room

Funky hairstyle

What is your least favorite word?

Doodle the shoes you are wearing

Zombie apocalypse

Dinosaurs at graduation

Giant hamster

Debbie Downer in your life

Favorite holiday

Who was your role model growing up?

If you could have any superpower...

Clown conference

Doodle your favorite, famous work of art

Your favorite day at work

Landmark from your state

Create a character using only triangular shapes

Your biggest
accomplishment

Alien birthday party

Skateboarding cowboys

Kite salesmen

Emotional eating utensils

Potato race

_____ themed parade

Awkward elevator ride

Magic staircase

Your biggest fear

Bubble blowing giants

Snails in a rock band

Fairytales

Never ending road trip

Your own candy land

Rabbits at a ballet recital

Living on the sun

Ballroom dancing reptiles

Biggest stressors

Weather

Best/funniest part of the day

Breakfast

Brightest Idea

Inspired by music

New invention

Futuristic transportation

Trip/Travels

Your emotions

Nature/ wildlife

Pirate

Inspired by book/movie

Robot

Words for robot noises

Illustrated nursery rhymes

Technology gone wrong

Pet's secret life

Aquarium

Dreams

Space travels

Time traveling

A new planet

Favorite dessert/party

Hot air balloon ride

Dream house

Your goals

Monsters under your bed

Tattoo sleeve

Your own city/ skyline

Anything interesting about your life

Fruit villains

Unlikely superheroes

Your definition of paradise

Garden

Lost at sea

Your own logo

Primitive Earth

It's raining_____

Animals in tuxedos

Walking food items

Traffic jam

End of the world

Evil plan

Favorite word

Volcano spewing out

_____

Farm animal's costume party

Insect infestation

Any thoughts

Nightly walk in the forest